W9-CNB-645

© 2009 White Star S.p.A.
Via Candido Sassone, 22/24
13100 Vercelli, Italy
www.whitestar.it

TRANSLATION: MARK MAHAN

ISBN 978-88-544-0441-0

REPRINTS:
1 2 3 4 5 6   13 12 11 10 09

Color separation: Fotomec, Turin
Printed in Thailand

WHITE STAR PUBLISHERS

"Our birthdays
are feathers
in the broad wing
of time"

Jean Paul Richter

*"The best birthdays of all
are those that haven't arrived yet"*

Robert Orben

Birthdays... ...under the spotlight

**Birthday cards... ...words and
thoughts of best wishes**

Cakes... and candles

Happy Birthday Cartoons

Rolling... ...Happy Birthday!

Animal Birthdays

Birthdays...

... UNDER THE SPOTLIGHT

Felicia Farr and Jack Lemmon { 8 February 1975 }

Kirk and Anne Douglas { April 1959 }

"It is lovely, when
I forget all
birthdays,
including my own,
to find that
somebody
remembers me"

- Ellen Glasgow -

**Errol Flynn, Nora Eddington,
Rita Hayworth and Orson Welles**

{ 1948 }

Charlie Chaplin { 16 April 1966 }

Maurice Chevalier and Haley Mills { 12 September 1961 }

Jane Fonda and Alain Delon { 8 November 1966 }

"YOU
CAN ONLY
PERCEIVE
REAL
BEAUTY IN
A PERSON
AS THEY
GET OLDER"

- Anouk Aimée -

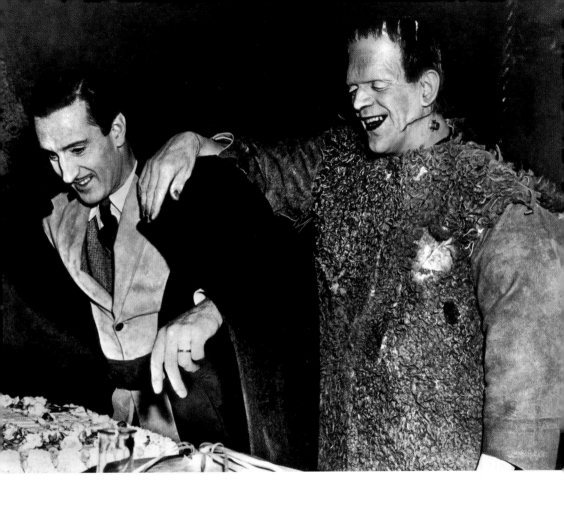

Basil Rathbone and Boris Karloff

{ 1939 }

Natalie Wood { 20 July 1959 }

Marilyn Monroe { 1 June 1956 }

"LET US
CELEBRATE THE
OCCASION WITH
WINE AND
SWEET WORDS"
- Plautus -

Johnny Hallyday and Sylvie Vartan

{ 15 August 1963 }

"You only live once, but if you do it right, once is enough"

- Joe Louis -

Joe Louis { 13 May 1941 }

Mick Jagger

Mick Jagger { 26 July 197

The Beatles { 7 July 1964 }

Julie Harris, The Beatles and Wilfred Brambell { March 1964 }

"I never think of the future. It comes soon enough"

- Albert Einstein -

Albert Einstein { 14 March 1951 }

Louis Armstrong

{ 4 August 1969 }

"WHAT WE PLAY IS LIFE"

- Louis Armstrong -

"YOU KNOW YOU ARE GETTING OLD
WHEN THE CANDLES COST
MORE THAN THE CAKE"

- Bob Hope -

Boris Karloff { 1968 }

B.B. King { 16 September 2005 }

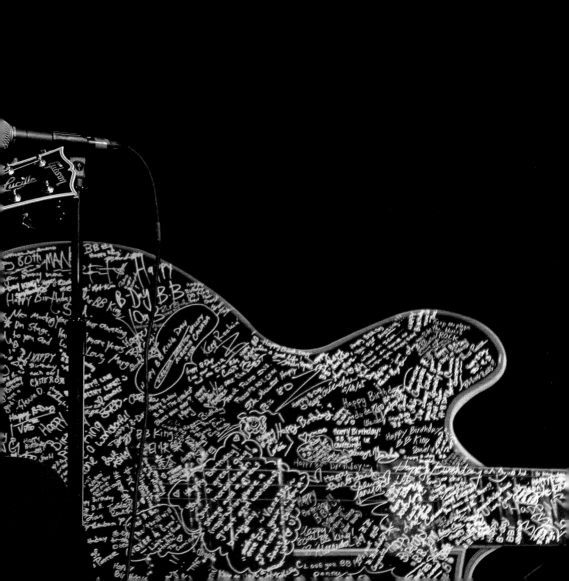

"Each ten years of a man's life has its own fortunes, its own hopes, its own desires"

- Johann Wolfgang Goethe -

Geordie Greig, Tamara Mellon and Sandra Choi :

10th anniversary of Jimmy Choo

{ September 2006 }

TATLER *celebrates* JIMMY CHOO'S 10th Anniversary

"MAP OUT YOUR FUTURE, BUT DO IT IN PENCIL. THE ROAD AHEAD IS AS LONG AS YOU MAKE IT"

- Jon Bon Jovi -

Jon Bon Jovi

{ 2 March 2008 }

Peter Ustinov { 16 April 1995 }

"Age is not measured by years. Some people are born old and tired while others are going strong at seventy"

- Dorothy Thompson -

Sophia Loren
{ 20 September 1994 }

"A WOMAN
IS ALWAYS
YOUNGER
THAN A MAN
OF EQUAL
YEARS"

- Elizabeth Barrett Browning -

Birthday cards...

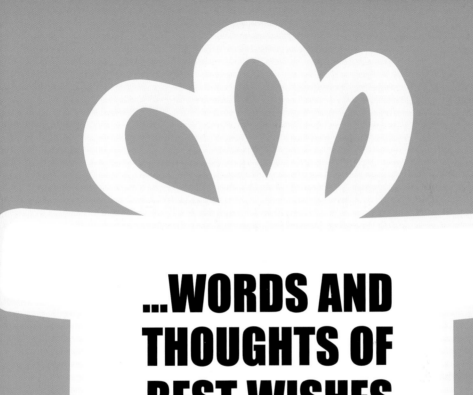

...WORDS AND
THOUGHTS OF
BEST WISHES

ein herzlicher Kuß.

Nicht aufdecken! es ist nicht von Nöthen,
Den Ihre Neugierde macht —
mich erröthen.

An affectionate kiss

"Don't uncover it! It's not necessary, because his curiosity makes me blush."

*My present
is a secret*

"Birthdays are good for you.
The more you have the longer you live"

- Anonymous -

Bilderbogen - Birthday of the King of the Dwarfs

{ Germany, 1880 }

el der Berge — Den König der Zwerge — Gebührend zu ehren — Mit herrlichen Beeren — Und süß ihm zu schmeicheln — Mit Schwämmen und Eicheln

lühendem Dorn — Und mit Kirschen und Korn! — Wie sie hastig sich mühen — Und schleppen und ziehen — Die niedlichen Buben — Gewaltige Ruben

Birnen und Schoten — Für ihren Despoten! — Das Geburtsfest zu feiern — Sie kommen mit Eiern — Mit Spargel und Nüssen — Und leckeren Bissen.

Das Bier aus em Durst — Salzbretzeln und Wurst — Daß Jeder denkt: Hätt' ich — Doch auch solche Jungen — Das wäre gelungen!" — Auch Fische und Krebs

Mother's birthday { Great Britain, 1893 }

Father's birthday { Great Britain, 1920 }

The first birthday

{ Allers *Family Journal*, February 1925 }

"YOUR BIRTHDAY IS A SPECIAL TIME TO CELEBRATE THE GIFT OF 'YOU' TO THE WORLD"

- Anonymous -

A happy birthday wish

{ Great Britain, 1895 }

"YOUTH
HAS NO AGE"

- Pablo Picasso -

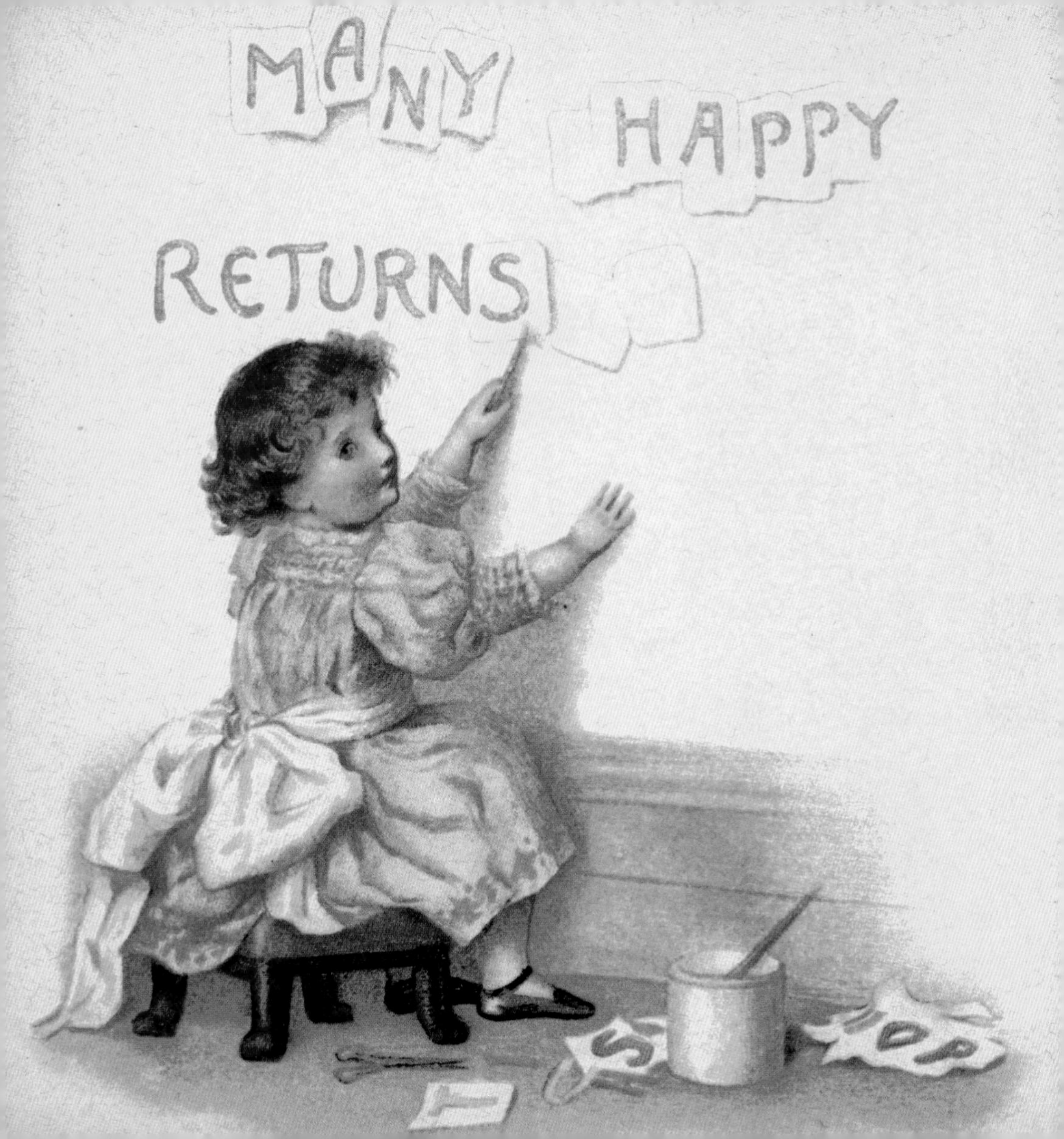
MANY HAPPY
RETURNS

Birthday card { 1916 }

Birthday card { Great Britain, 1880 }

Illustration by Lisa Berkshire

Illustration by Linda Bronson

"I never forget my wife's birthday.

It's usually the day after she reminds me about it"

- Anonymous -

Exchanging gifts

Cakes...
and Candles

BIRTHDAY WISHES FOR ALL TASTES

"AN ANNIVERSARY IS A TIME TO CELEBRATE THE JOYS OF TODAY, THE MEMORIES OF YESTERDAY, AND THE HOPES OF TOMORROW"

- Anonymous -

150 years of Louis Vuitton { November 2004 }

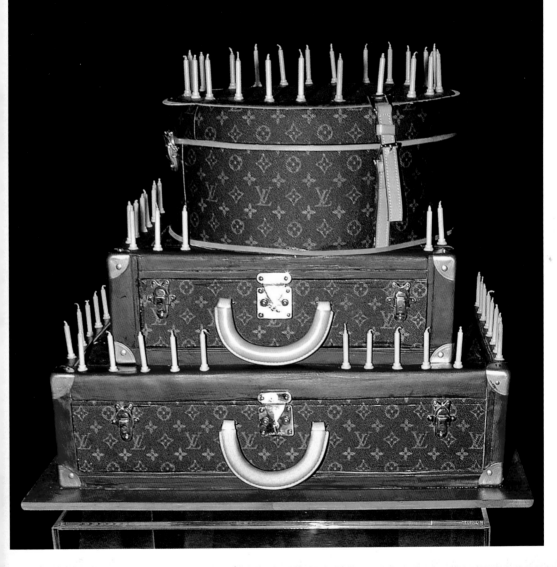

A giant cake prepared for the occasion of Queen Charlotte's Birthday Ball { May 1930 }

"Birthdays are
nature's way of
telling us to eat
more cake"

- *Anonymous* -

70 years for the Eiffel Tower

{ January 1959 }

"YOUTH IS THE GIFT OF NATURE, BUT AGE IS A WORK OF ART"

- Garson Kanin -

The centennial of the Marshall Field department stores { January 1952 }

50 years of the Waldorf-Astoria Hotel, New York { September 1981 }

"All the world
is birthday cake,
so take a piece,
but not too much."

- It's all too much, The Beatles -

The first anniversary of the film,
"Around the World in 80 Days"

{ October 1957 }

"The first 100 years are the hardest"

- Wilson Mizner -

150 years of the Plaza Hotel, New York

{ October 2007 }

"IF YOU
SURVIVE
LONG
ENOUGH,
YOU'RE
REVERED -
RATHER LIKE
AN OLD
BUILDING"

- Katherine Hepburn -

**Queen Elisabeth the II cuts the cake at the celebration
of Alberta's Centennial, Alberta, Canada**

{ May 2005 }

"Don't just count
  your years,
  make your
  years count"

- Ernest Meyers -

**First anniversary of
the reign of King
Mohammed VI of Morocco**

{ July 2000 }

Tenth anniversary of the "Today" show on NBC { January 2007 }

Centennial of the department store KaDeWe, Berlin { March 2007 }

"DISNEYLAND WILL NEVER
BE COMPLETED. IT WILL
CONTINUE TO GROW AS LONG
AS THERE IS IMAGINATION
LEFT IN THE WORLD"

- Walt Disney -

First anniversary of the Paris Disneyland

{ April 1993 }

happy
birthday

CARTOONS

"If a person gives you
his time, he can give you
no more precious gift"

- Frank Tyger -

The Tigger Movie

{ 2000 }

Sleeping Beauty

{ 1959 }

Alice in Wonderland

{ 1951 }

Image from the cartoon "The Little Lulu Show" { 1995 }

Garfield celebrates his 10th birthday { May 1988 }

"THERE ARE
364 DAYS
WHEN YOU
MIGHT GET
UN-BIRTHDAY
PRESENTS
AND ONLY
ONE FOR
BIRTHDAY
PRESENTS"

- Lewis Carroll -

Rugrats, Tommy's first birthday

{ 1991 }

Simon:
"Dave's coming back soon, Alvin, and we need to get him a present!"

Alvin and the Chipmunks, Dave's birthday { 1983 }

Madagascar { 2005 }

"There is still
no cure for
the common
birthday"

- *John Glenn* -

ROLLING...

...Happy Birthday!

"Age is not
a particularly
interesting subject.
Anyone can get old.
All you have to do
is live long enough"

- Groucho Marx -

Early To Bed

{ 1928 }

Dreaming that it's your birthday and no one remembers to wish you a happy birthday, can that be classified as a nightmare?

Nightmare

{ 1964 }

A Streetcar named Desire { 1951 }

St. Martin's Lane { 1938 }

"NEARLY ALL THE BEST THINGS
THAT CAME TO ME IN LIFE
HAVE BEEN UNEXPECTED,
UNPLANNED BY ME"

- Carl Sandburg -

How to Murder Your Wife

{ 1965 }

"I'll never be old.
To me, old age is
always 15 years older
than I am"

- Bernard M. Baruch -

Chitty Chitty Bang Bang

{ 1968 }

"The advantage of being eighty years old is that one has had many people to love"

- *Jean Renoir* -

The Lord of the Rings : The Fellowship of the Ring

{ 2001 }

"You're only young once
but you can be
immature forever"

- John Greier -

The Longest Yard

{ 2005 }

"The secret to staying young is to live honestly, eat slowly, and lie about your age"

- Lucille Ball -

The Flintstones

{ 1994 }

Boys On The Side

{ 1995 }

Working Girl

{ 1988 }

"If you carry your childhood with you you never become older"

- Abraham Sutzkever -

Alfie

{ 2004 }

Day Watch
{ 2006 }

"IT IS NEVER TOO LATE TO HAVE A HAPPY CHILDHOOD"

- Tom Robbins -

Animal
BIRTHDAYS

"THE TRICK IS GROWING UP WITHOUT GROWING OLD"

- Casey Stengel -

Cheeta celebrates his 75th birthday

{ April 2007 }

He has the memory of an elephant. **That's the reason whay I always turn to him to remind me of birthdays.**

Ruth the elephant celebrates her 30th birthday

{ April 1926 }

After all, what are birthdays?

**Today they're
here, tomorrow
they're gone**

Pete the hippopotamus on the day of his 44th birthday

{ July 1947 }

President Warren G. Harding's dog,
Laddie Boy, with a birthday cake

{ July 1922 }

Never look a gift horse in the mouth.

W.K. Kellogg with a pair of twin Arabian colts

{ 1940 }

"MY
ROOMMATE
GOT A PET
ELEPHANT.
THEN IT
GOT LOST.
IT'S IN THE
APARTMENT
SOMEWHERE"

- Steven Wright -

A baby elephant at a birthday party for children

{ 1960 }

photographic credits

Page 12 Everett Collection/Contrasto **Page 13** Bettmann/Corbis **Pages 14-15** Frank Cronenweth/The Kobal Collection **Page 16** Tramonto/Agefotostock/Marka **Page 17** Rue des Archives **Pages 18-19** Keystone/Getty Images **Page 21** Universal/The Kobal Collection **Page 22** Murray Garrett/Getty Images **Page 23** Bettmann/Corbis **Page 25** James Andanson/Sygma/Corbis **Page 27** Everett Collection/Contrasto **Pages 29, 30** Bettmann/Corbis **Page 31** Evening Standard/Hulton Archive/Getty Images **Page 33** Bettmann/Corbis **Page 34** Everett Collection/Contrasto **Page 37** Dmitri Kessel/Time & Life Pictures/Getty Images **Pages 38-39** Gene Blevins/Corbis **Page 41** Dave M. Benett/Getty Images **Page 43** William Thomas Cain/Getty Images **Page 45** David Lefranc/Kipa/Corbis **Page 47** SipaPress/Olycom **Pages 50-51 e 53** Interfoto Pressebildagentur/Alamy **Pages 54, 55, 57, 59** Mary Evans Picture Library **Page 60** SuperStock/Agefotostock/Marka **Page 61** Mary Evans Picture Library **Page 62** Lisa Berkshire/Illustration Works/Corbis **Page 63, 65** Images.com/Corbis **Page 69** Regis Martin/Getty Images **Pages 70-71** Fox Photos/Getty Images **Page 73** Roger Viollet/Archivio Alinari **Page 74** Ralph Crane/Time & Life Pictures/Getty Images **Pages 75, 76-77** Bettmann/Corbis **Page 79** Getty Images **Page 81** AP/LaPresse **Pages 82-83** Patrick Robert/Corbis Sygma/Corbis **Page 84, 85** AP/LaPresse **Page 87** Pascal Della Zuana/Corbis Sygma/Corbis **Pages 90-91** Walt Disney Pictures/Album/Contrasto **Page 92** Walt Disney Productions/Album/Contrasto **Page 93** Walt Disney Pictures/Album/Contrasto **Pages 94, 95** Everett Collection/Contrasto **Page 97** Klasky-Csupo/courtesy Everett Collection/Contrasto **Page 99** Everett Collection/Contrasto **Pages 100-101, 102-103** DreamWorks/courtesy Everett Collection/Contrasto **Pages 106-107** The Koball Collection **Page 109** Everett Collection/Contrasto **Page 110** Warner Bros/The Kobal Collection **Page 111** Associated British/The Kobal Collection **Page 113** Roger Viollet/Archivio Alinari **Pages 114-115, 117** Everett Collection/Contrasto **Pages 118-119** Tracy Bennett/Happy Madison Prods/Paramount Pictures/The Kobal Collection **Page 121** Everett Collection/Contrasto **Page 122** Suzanne Hanover/Canal +/Regency/Alcor/The Kobal Collection **Page 123** 20th Century Fox Film Corp/courtesy Everett Collection/Contrasto **Page 125** Paramount Pictures/Album/Contrasto **Page 127** Channel One/Tabbak/The Kobal Collection **Page 131** Frederic Neema/Gamma/Eyedea Presse/Contrasto **Pages 133, 135, 136** Bettmann/Corbis **Page 137** Corbis **Page 139** Bettmann/Corbis **Page 141** David Lewis Hodgson/Mary Evans Picture Library